Fast Guitar Chord Transitions

A Beginner's Guide to Moving Quickly Between Guitar Chords Like a Professional

MICAH BROOKS

© 2020 | WorshipHeart Publishing
All Rights Reserved.

Also By Micah Brooks

The Guitar Authority Series:

Worship Guitar In Six Weeks:
A Complete Beginner's Guide to Learning
Rhythm Guitar for Christian Worship Music

42 Guitar Chords Everyone Should Know:
A Complete Step-By-Step Guide To Mastering
42 Of The Most Important Guitar Chords

Guitar Secrets Revealed:
Unconventional and Amazing Guitar Chords,
Professional Techniques, Capo Tricks,
Alternate Tunings, Head Math, Rhythm & More

The Piano Authority Series:

Piano Chords One (All Seven Natural Keys):
A Beginner's Guide To Simple Music Theory
and Playing Chords To Any Song Quickly

Piano Chords Two (All Flat and Sharp Keys):
A Beginner's Guide To Simple Music Theory
and Playing Chords To Any Song Quickly

Songbooks and Music:

Micah Brooks All Things New EP Songbook

Micah Brooks All Things New EP

Christian Books:

Forsaking All Others:
The book we wish we'd had when dating, engaged, and in the early years of our marriage to set us up for future success.

21 Day Character Challenge:
A Daily Devotional and Bible Reading Plan

Galatians: A Fresh, New Six Day
Bible Study and Commentary

Ephesians: A Fresh, New Six Day
Bible Study and Commentary

James: A Fresh, New Five Day
Bible Study and Commentary

Micah Brooks

Copyright Information

Published by WorshipHeart Publishing

© 2020 Micah Brooks Kennedy | WorshipHeart Publishing

All rights herein, both implied and expressed, are reserved. No part of this book may be reproduced or transmitted in any form without prior written consent from WorshipHeart Publishing. This includes any means electronic or mechanical, such as photocopying. Violators will be prosecuted.

For written permission contact WorshipHeart Publishing at: worshippublishing.com or email: worshippublishing@worshippublishing.com

Cover Design by Micah Brooks Kennedy

Dedication

It's my honor to dedicate this book to my second-grade teacher, Rich Campbell. You had an acoustic guitar in your classroom and I fell in love with the instrument. Thank you for making that available to me and being overjoyed when I would come back to class having learned something new on my own at home. Your graciousness and patience with my little eight-year-old music brain will forever be pleasant in my memory.

Micah Brooks

Contents

Introduction	9
The Chords in "G"	13
The Chords in "D"	25
The Chords in "C"	35
The Chords in "E"	45
The Chords in "A"	51
The Nashville Numbers System and the Mighty Capo	59
Closing Thoughts and Finding Songs to Play	71
About The Author	73
Connect With Micah Brooks	75

Micah Brooks

Introduction

The secret to transitioning guitar chords quickly is here!

As a guitar teacher of more than fifteen years, it's fun to see complete beginners learn their first couple of chords. Most of the time these are the G, D, Em, and C chords. Maybe you have already learned these? You can play most Taylor Swift songs with these four in your arsenal and a capo. We'll talk about the capo at the end of this book–a most useful tool indeed.

Everyone can learn to play those four chords on their own. With the invention of YouTube and the internet, paying for beginner guitar lessons is no longer needed. At least, this is how I feel. As a teacher, I've set about to training my new guitarists by thinking through ways to be quicker, stronger, better. I want my lessons to be ones where the student gets far more than they ever would using an online resource. One of those advantages to in-person lessons with me is that I teach the all important guitar chord *transitions* along with the chords themselves.

If you've tried to learn guitar before you've likely spent time delving through all the basic beginner chords. What is a G; how to play an A major; and so on. Where the rubber meets the road is when you want to use your chords to play your favorite songs. How often have you placed your fingers in the G chord shape trying to play along with the radio all the while the G has passed and it's time for the D? But you just got your fingers into the G shape! Ugh!

I'll show you the nifty secrets and tricks that give you the tools you'll need to transition your chords so quickly that you'll be bored waiting for the D chord to come around because you can get to it so quickly. These are methods and rules you can use to speed up every chord transition you make. This book shows you the way professionals guitarists think.

Chord Diagram

Each chord in this book has a unique diagram. There are several parts to each one. Refer back to this section as you begin learning.

Chord Diagram Explained

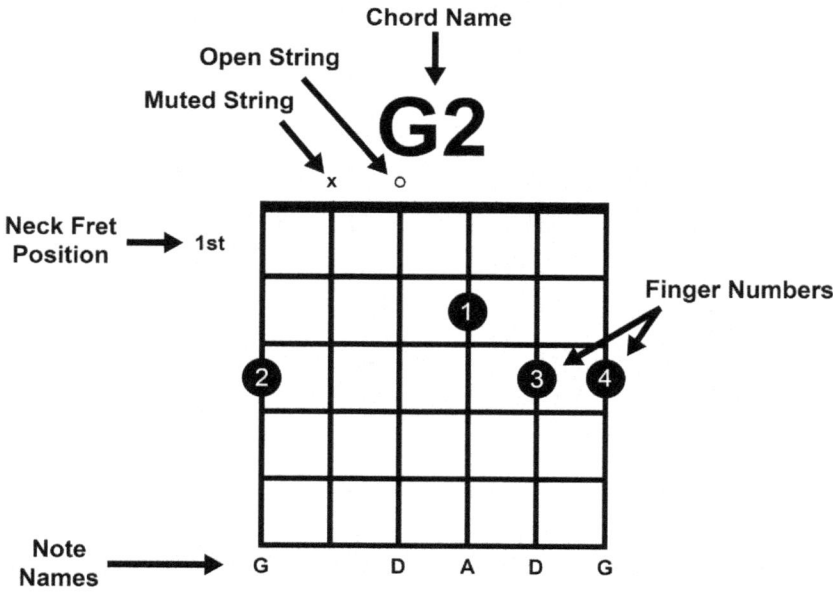

Chord Name

This section gives you the name of the chord. This may include a chord suffix, like C6 where the "6" is at the end and is a modifier.

Open String

An open string is a guitar string that is played with no finger touching it. The note name is the string's name. For example, if you play an open fourth string (like in this G2 chord example), the open note being played on the D string (4) is a "D".

Muted String

A muted string is one that is either being muted by a neighboring finger or intentionally not being played with the right, strumming hand. In this example of the G2 chord, the A string (5) is not played.

Neck Fret Position

The neck fret position number is important to always notice when reviewing a chord diagram. That number signifies the starting position of your fingers on the guitar neck. It can go as high as the last fret on the upper part of your guitar neck. If you see a "1st" denotation, then the chord is played in open position at the beginning of the neck. "1st" is the *home base* position on the guitar. Everything else is related to that home base position. Were you to see "7th", like in an E chord, then your root note begins on the fourth fret. Do your best to observe the neck fret position indication for each chord.

Finger Numbers

While you could use nicknames for each finger on your left hand (like your index finger, pinky, etc.) most guitar teachers will use numbers per finger. Using numbers allows for quick reference for chord diagrams and transitioning.

Here is how I detail each finger of the left hand. The index finger is (1). Your middle finger is (2), ring finger is (3), and pinky finger (4). I label the thumb (T). While you will not get into any thumb playing in this book, you may as you improve in your skills moving on to further chording. Note: left-handed guitarists will use the opposite hand, making each of the labels above true for the *right hand* rather than your left.

Note Names

Below each chord diagram are the note names being played per string. Please notice that these are not the root names of the strings. Rather, these are the notes being played after fretting the chord. Some of the notes will be the open notes, but only when there is no finger needed for that particular string in the chord. When a string is being omitted or muted, no note name will be present.

It's time to dive in! Let's go!

The Chords in "G"
You can play just about any song using this key

Before we even set sail, the purpose of this book is to teach you how to transition between guitar chords that you likely already know, but to do so faster. These are techniques that the professionals use that you may not have considered. While I do believe you can also learn these chords if you haven't tried before, I do recommend you consider my first book in this series, *Worship Guitar In Six Weeks*. In that one, you'll learn fingerings for each chord. It's built as a step by step guide. However, if you forgo that book, you will likely still be able to learn your new chords using the steps described here, but they won't be described in as much detail as in that other book. This book is about speedy transitions.

We cannot make any chord transitions until we have a chord fretted on our guitar. Then we can make our transition to the next chord. Let's begin with a standard G chord. Even if you haven't played this specific version of G before, I recommend using this fingering.

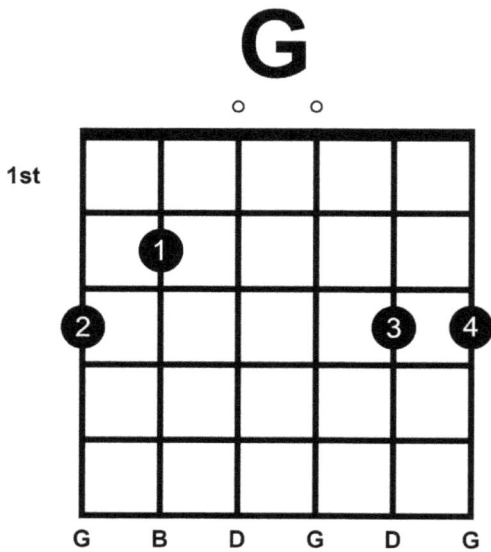

Moving from G to D

Let's transition to our next chord. Often you will move from a G to a D chord. One of the tricks that makes transitioning super fast is to find a pivot point. A pivot point is any finger on a string and fret that stay the same for both chords. For this instance, the third (3) finger on the third fret of the second string (B) doesn't move. Every other finger must move. Let's use that third (3) finger as our pivot point. Fret the G chord and follow these quick steps to get to the D.

Begin your transition by taking every finger off the neck of your guitar except for your third (3) finger. Now the only finger left on your guitar is your third (3) finger.

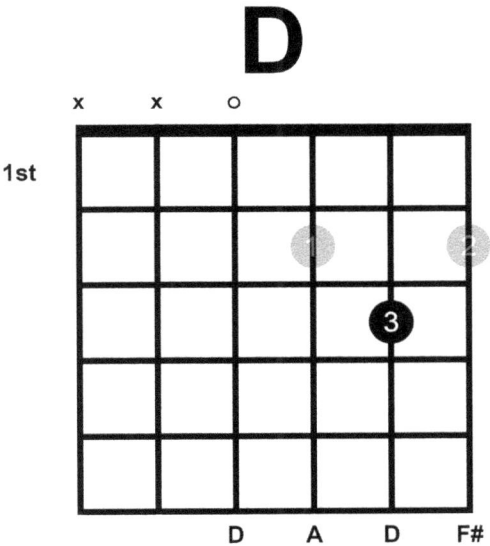

Moving both fingers at the same time, bring your first (1) finger and your second (2) finger into their places on the third (G) and first (e) strings, respectively. You want them to move simultaneously for the quickest transition.

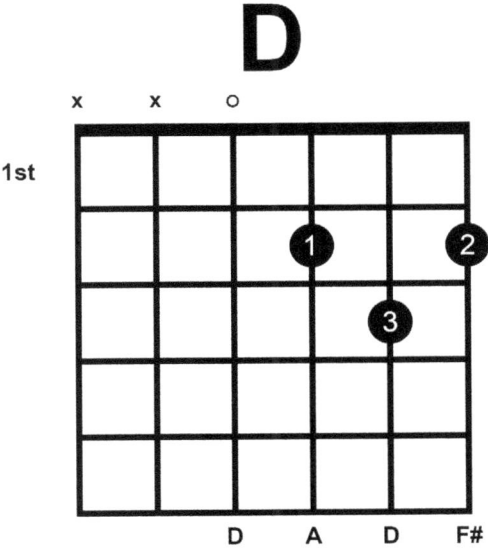

Try going back to the G chord and transition again to the D using our steps. Once you begin to feel confident in this transition you'll find that there is no down time between chords. To get back to G quickly, make sure that you leave your third (3) finger on the third fret of the second string (B) at all times. Your other three fingers should move in one motion back to the G by using that third fret as your pivot point. How fast can you switch between each chord?

G to Cadd9

Another typical transition you will find in the key of G is moving from a G chord to a Cadd9, which is also known as a C2. While it is extremely easy, here are the steps. First, fret a G chord. Keep your third (3) and fourth (4) fingers in place, but lift your first (1) and second (2) fingers simultaneously.

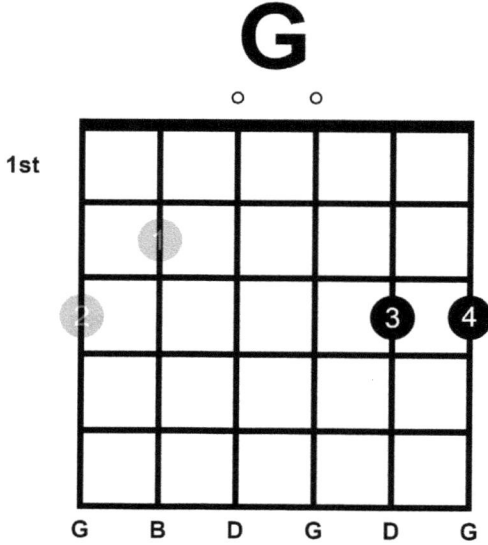

Fast Guitar Chord Transitions

To get to the Cadd9, simply place your first (1) and second (2) fingers onto the next strings over. Each finger should move together and settle in on the fifth (A) and fourth (D) strings at the same time. This makes the chord transition quite fast.

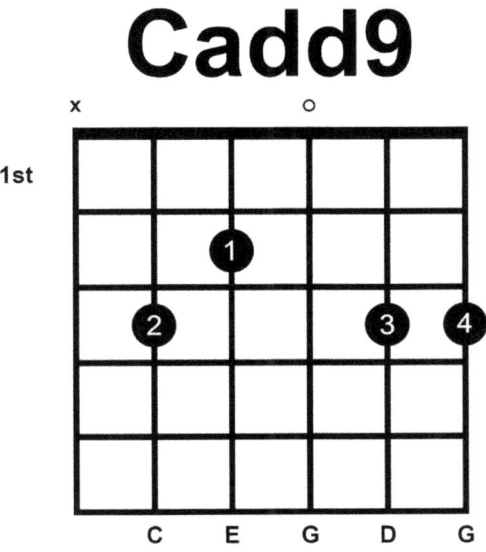

You can even move back and forth between Cadd9 and G to practice this transition until you can move three or four times in two seconds. You should be that fast!

Micah Brooks

G to Em7

One of the coolest sounding guitar chord transitions is between the G and Em7 chords. You may have only played an Em to this point in your guitar life. If this is the case, this Em7 chord will be one of the best new things you learn in this book. First, fret a G chord. To make the transition, leave your first (1), third (3), and fourth (4) fingers in place, but lift your second (2) finger.

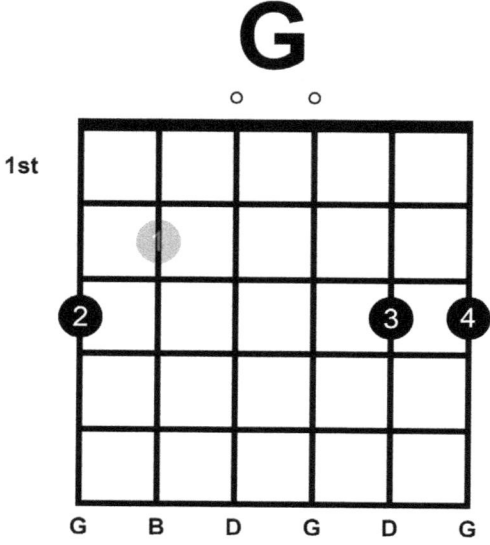

Next, place your second (2) finger on the second fret of the fourth string (D). The transition is that simple. When you strum all six strings of an Em7 after coming from a G chord it sounds rich. You may notice that your first (1) finger may need to rise slightly to let your second (2) finger make its move. This is normal. I recommend attempting to minimize how much you need to lift that finger. It shouldn't come off the guitar string but only loosen enough to let the other finger in.

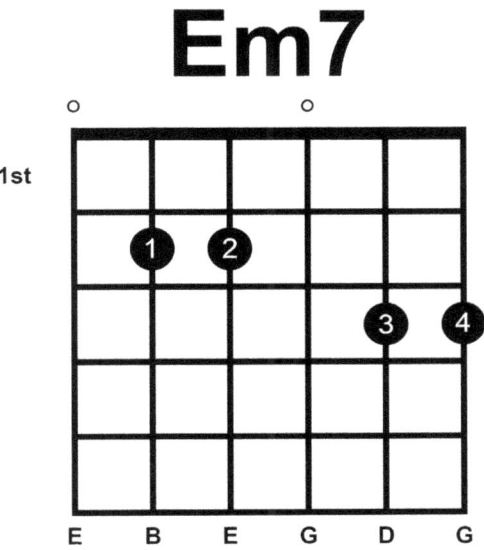

Practice going back and forth between G and Em7.

Micah Brooks

Cadd9 to D

You will often move the Cadd9 chord to a D while playing in the key of G. Much like moving from G to D, the third (3) finger is your pivot point. Begin by fretting the Cadd9 chord. Next, take every finger off the neck of the guitar except for the third (3) finger–again, this is your pivot point.

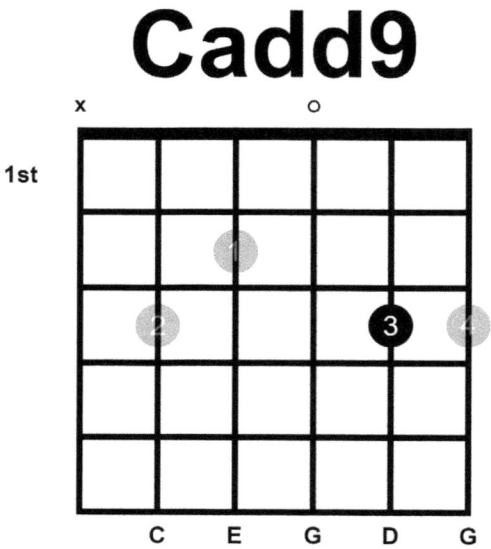

Using that pivot point, move your first (1) and second (2) fingers into place in one motion. Practice going between Cadd9 and D using your third (3) finger pivot point.

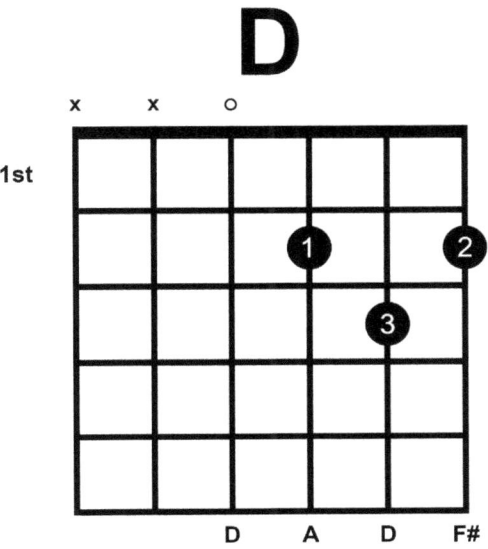

G to Am

Moving from any chord in the key of G to an Am can be tricky. It's because Am doesn't share any pivot points with any of the other chords. That said, there is a method that I use to fret an Am quickly. First, fret a G chord. This is often one of the chords you will come from when going to an Am.

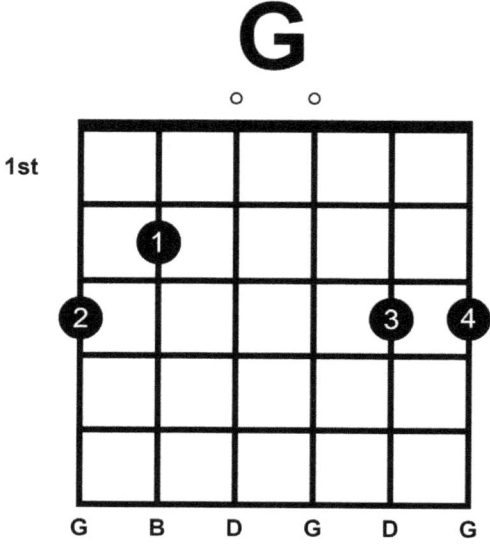

Every finger will come off the guitar for this transition. When placing your fingers for the Am, the trick is to do so using the right series. To begin, moving together, place your second (2) and third (3) fingers onto the second frets of the fourth (D) and third (G) strings. Again, you want both fingers to move simultaneously.

Fast Guitar Chord Transitions

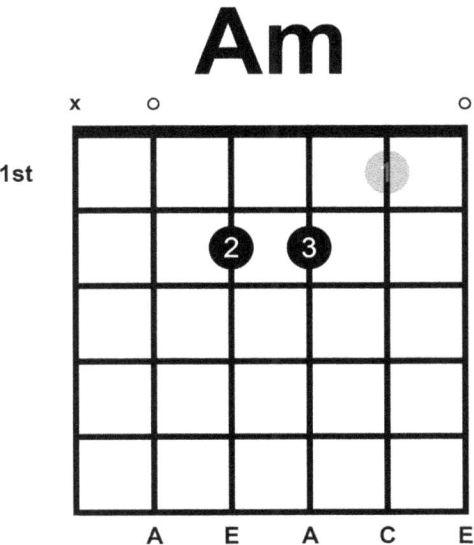

Your final finger to move is your first (1) finger. It must sneak behind the other two fingers that are already in place. You'll now have a quick transition to the Am.

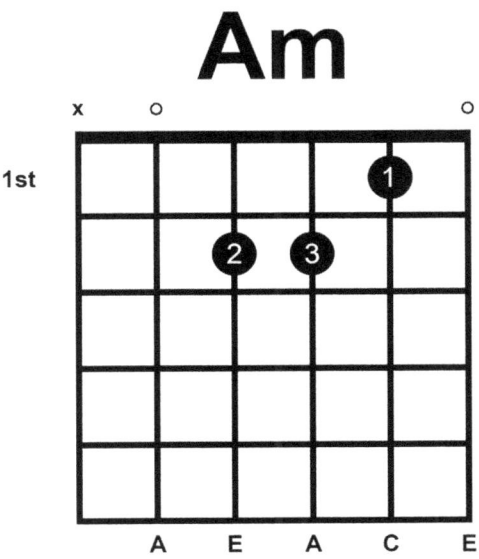

Practice moving between G and Am. You should also practice transitioning from the other chords in G, such as moving D to Am, Cadd9 to Am, and so on.

It's time to move on to the next key, which is the key of D. You're ready!

The Chords in "D"

The key of D is one of the most pleasant sounding keys to play in on the guitar

The key of D is unique for the guitar in that it has three different chords that have open strings as their root notes. Those are D, A, and Em. Each chord beginning with those open strings makes for greater resonance which creates a better tone. Let's learn how to transition between some of the most popular chords in the key of D.

Moving from D to G

When you moved from G to D in the first chapter you took off your first (1) and second (2) fingers to move them to the D chord. Now we are going to work in reverse. Fret a D chord.

Micah Brooks

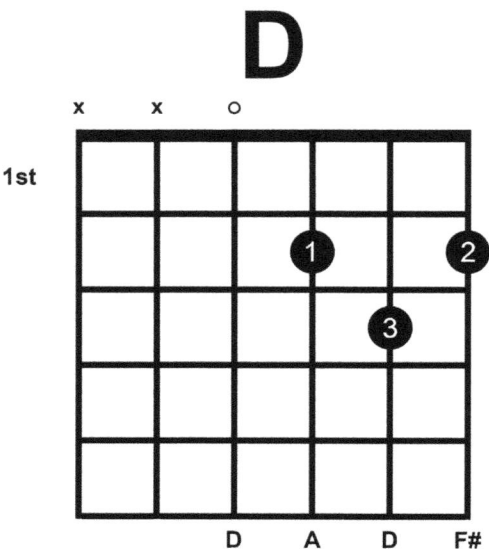

You will remove your first (1) and second (2) fingers while putting down your fourth (4) finger on the third fret of the first (e) string.

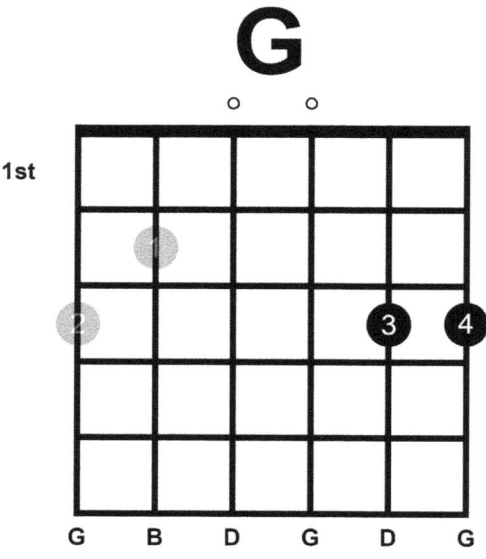

Fast Guitar Chord Transitions

Finally, in one motion, move your first (1) and second (2) fingers onto the sixth (E) string third fret and the fifth (A) string second fret. Try to be as seamless in this motion as possible.

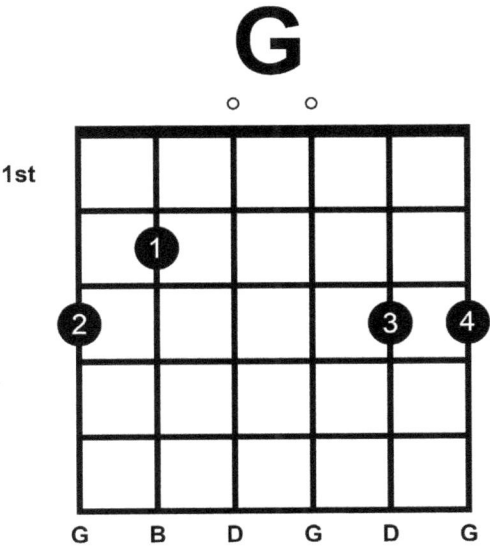

Micah Brooks

Moving from D to A

Another chord transition you'll make often is going from D to A. There is a finger sliding trick you can use. First, fret a D chord.

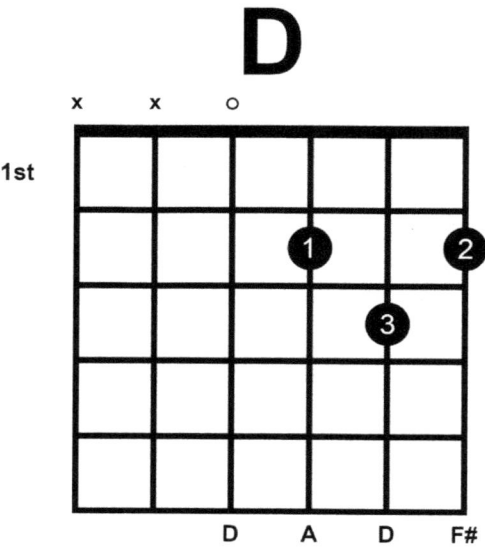

Take both your first (1) and second (2) fingers off the guitar, but keep them close together. This leaves your third (3) finger still on the third fret of the second (B) string.

Fast Guitar Chord Transitions

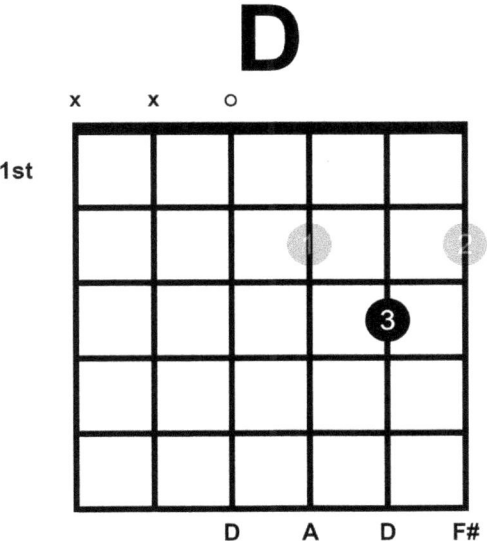

Now, slide your third (3) finger down one fret on the second (B) string. Your third (3) finger should now be on the second fret. This slide is similar to a pivot point, only you'll need to move that finger down a fret.

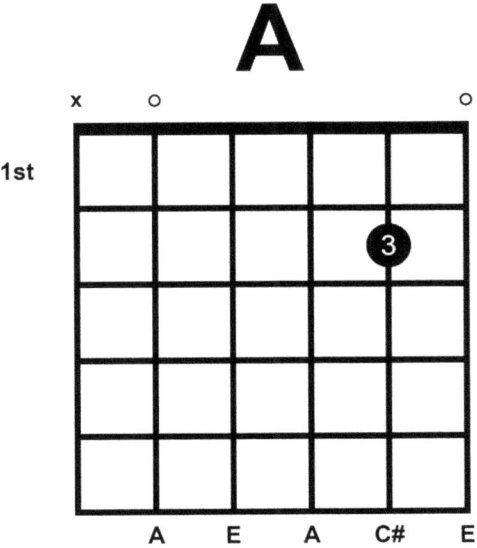

Last, simultaneously add your first (1) and second (2) fingers onto the second frets of the fourth (D) and third (G) strings. If you haven't played an A chord before moving all of your fingers in a line on the second frets of those strings may feel hard or even impossible. I promise that it is very doable, but you have to work to get all three fingers into a tight package.

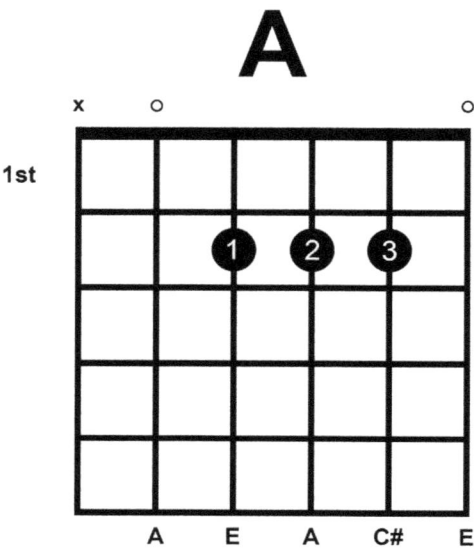

Moving from A to Bm

While there is no easy trick to get you from A to Bm, there is still a method that I use that could prove helpful for you. First, fret your A chord again.

Fast Guitar Chord Transitions

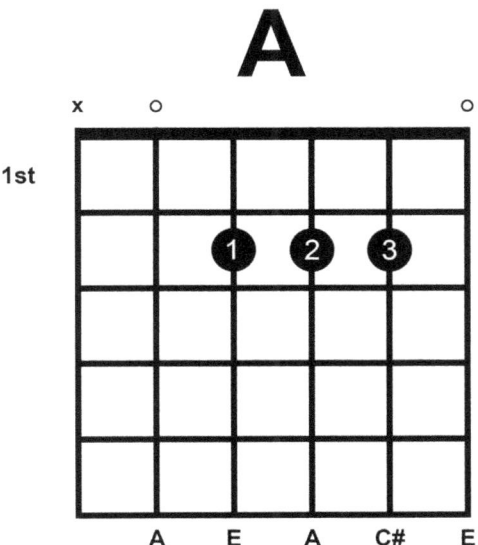

You will now take every finger off the guitar, but do it in this sequence as you move to Bm. Let your first (1) and second (2) finger come straight up and let them hover above the strings. Your third (3) finger will now meet with your fourth (4) finger that wasn't used in your A chord. You'll need it for the Bm. Both should move together onto the fourth frets of the fourth (D) and third (G) strings.

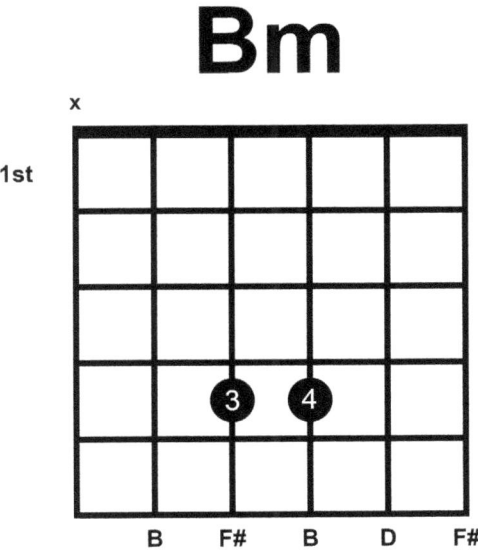

In one motion place your first (1) and second (2) fingers on the second and third frets of the fifth (A) and second (B) strings respectively. It's important that you do this in one motion to make a tough transition more smooth. Please notice that your first (1) finger forms a barre across the second fret. If you've never played this type of chord it will be difficult at first. Practice will definitely make perfect. You may even notice some soreness in that first (1) finger. Push through! It gets easier!

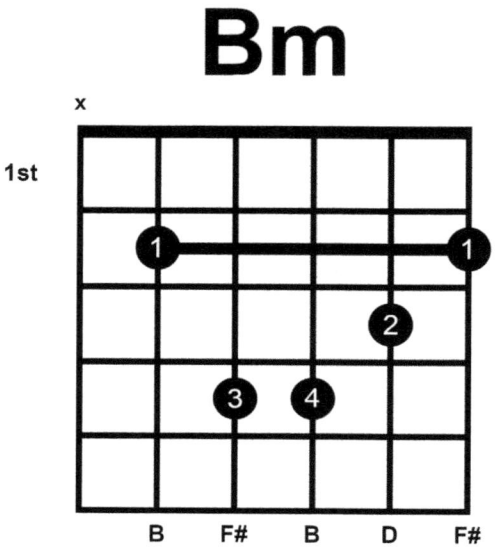

Moving from Bm to Em

While you have a Bm fretted you can move to an Em chord easily. There are two quick steps. First, take all fingers off of your guitar except for the first (1) finger. While playing the Bm chord, your first (1) finger was barring across the second fret of five strings. You will not need that barre any longer. Rather, leave only your first (1) finger on the second fret of the fifth (A) string.

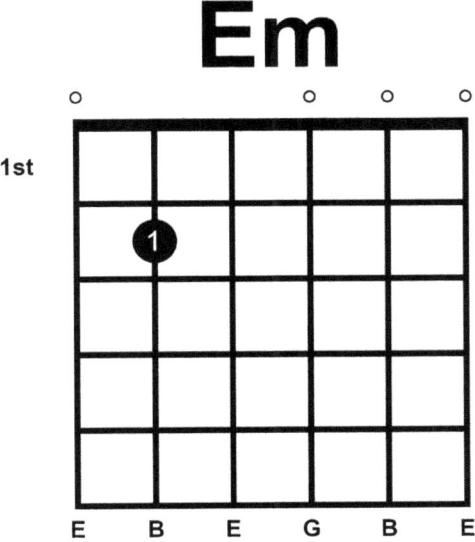

Now place your second (2) finger on the second fret of the fourth (D) string.

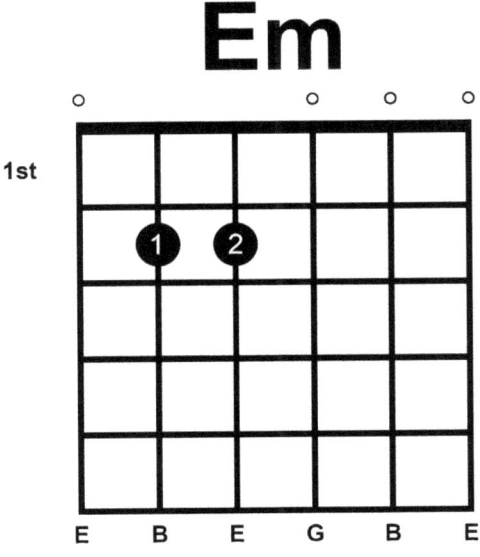

Getting from Bm to Em is easy. However, moving from Em to Bm requires a lot more movement. Treat it much like you did when moving to Bm from A. First move your third (3) and fourth (4) fingers in place. Then build your barre on the second fret while simultaneously fretting the third fret of the second (B) string with your second (2) finger. Practice this transition often. Muscle memory will eventually take over.

The Chords in "C"

A bit more difficult, but the benefits of playing in the key of C are worth it!

You have likely learned a C chord early on in guitar lessons. Let's look at some practical ways to get to and from the most important chords in this key. This will include moving from C to Am, Dm, Gsus, and an easy F chord that everyone should know!

C to Am

One of the most often used transitions in the key of C is moving from C to Am. It's easy! Plus, it sounds great! First, fret a C chord.

Micah Brooks

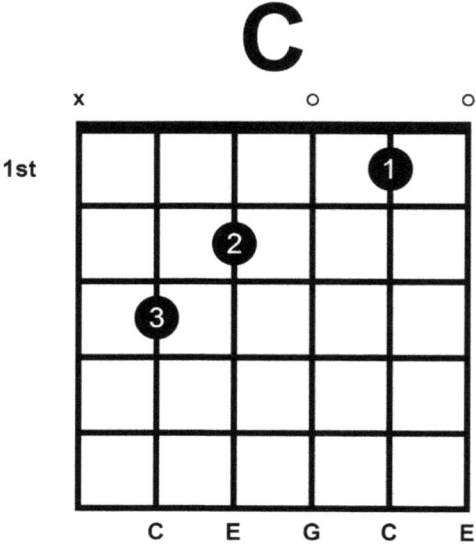

To get from C to Am you'll need to move your third (3) finger from the fifth (A) string to the second fret of the third (G) string. Practice making this transition over and over.

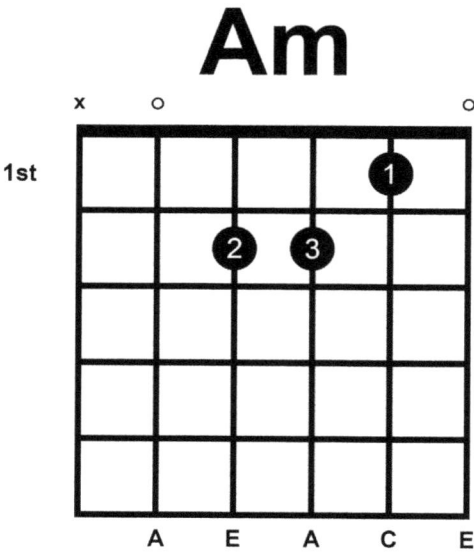

Am to Dm

Moving from Am to Dm is a unique transition in that it can be done in one quick motion. Moving less than all three fingers at once is inefficient. Here are the steps. First, fret an Am.

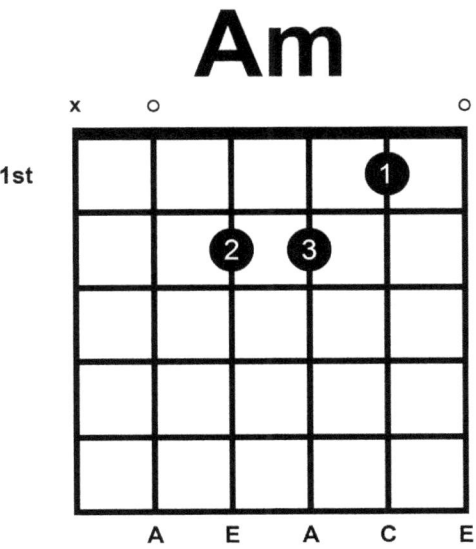

Now move all three fingers from Am to Dm. Your order of second (2), third (3), and first (1) fingers will remain the same, but the frets will be slightly different for your third (3) finger. You'll move it up from the second fret of the second (B) string to the third fret. All other fingers simply move over one string each but remain on the same fret numbers.

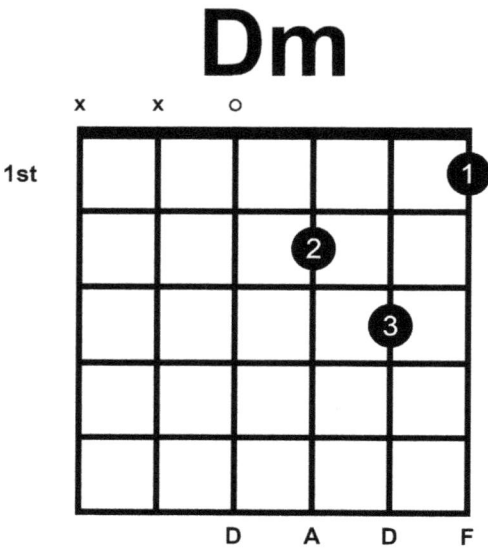

C to Gsus and open G

Typically during the first few guitar lessons someone takes will lead to learning a C and G chord that look nothing alike. There is an easier way to shift from C to G. There is also a great way to move from a C to a nice sounding chord called Gsus. The *sus* stands for *suspended*. It's slightly different in the playing and sound of a G chord. Fret a C chord.

Fast Guitar Chord Transitions

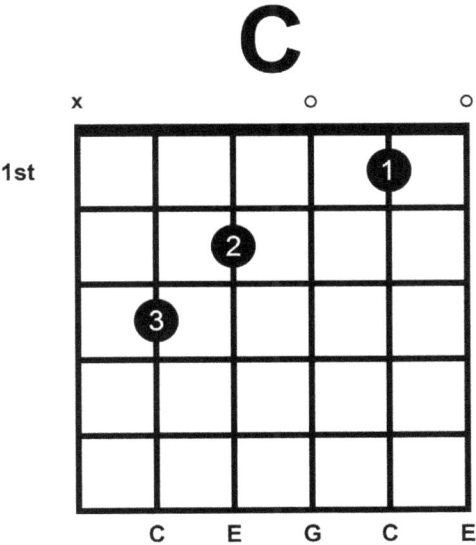

Move your second (2) and third (3) fingers in the same fingering positions to the sixth (G) and fifth (A) strings. This should happen in one easy motion. Now take your first (1) finger off the neck of the guitar, but only enough for it to hover over your strings.

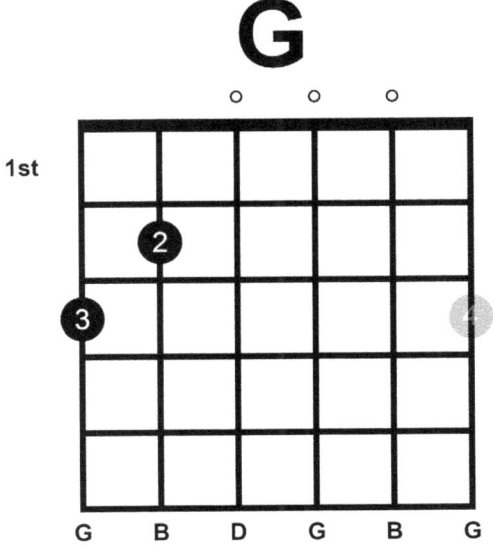

Last, add your fourth (4) finger on the first (e) string. Strum all six strings. This is a new way to play a G chord. Practice the transition to and from these chords to make it quick.

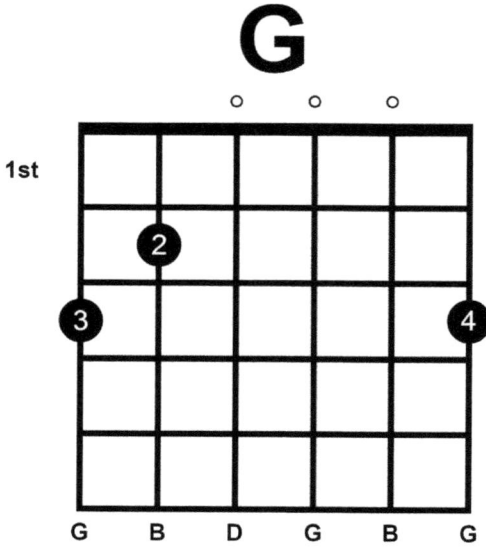

To build a Gsus chord you only need to put your first (1) finger down on the first fret of the second (B) string. This is the finger that is hovering just above this fret. Also, gently lift your second (2) finger so that it mutes the fifth (A) string. Strum across all six strings. Practice going to and from C to Gsus. You will get faster each time.

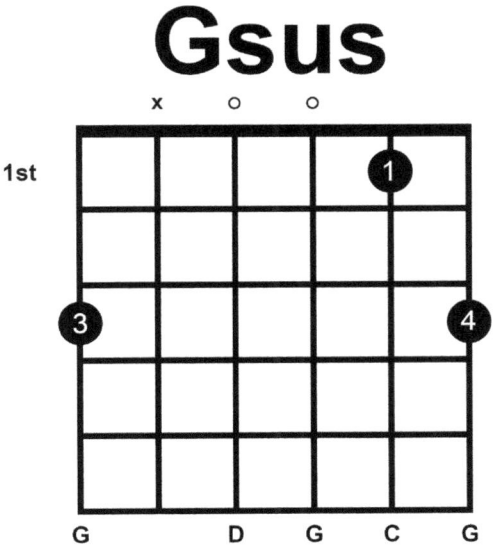

C to Easy F

While this may be a review for you, I'd like to walk you through transitioning quickly from a C chord to an easy way to play F. You have likely learned the full barre chord F. See it below.

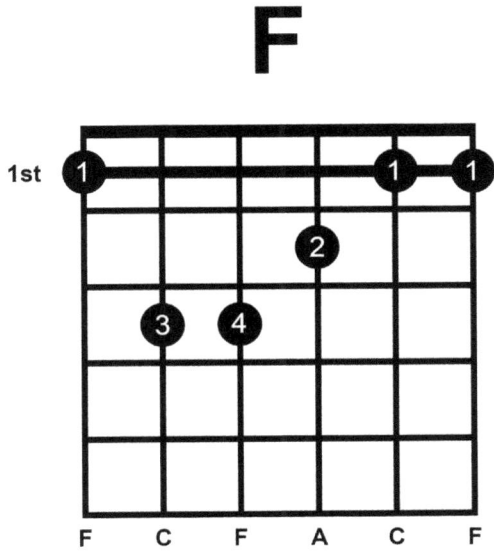

There is an easier way to play F that is only four strings rather than all six. It still requires a barre with the first (1) finger, but it's only across two strings rather than all six. First, fret a C chord.

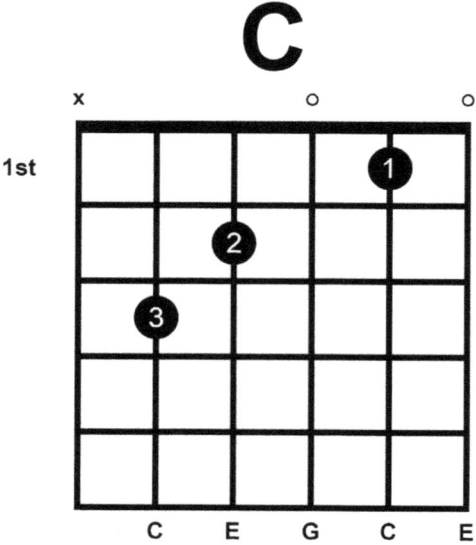

To get to F you'll need to first barre the first strings of the second (B) and first (e) strings.

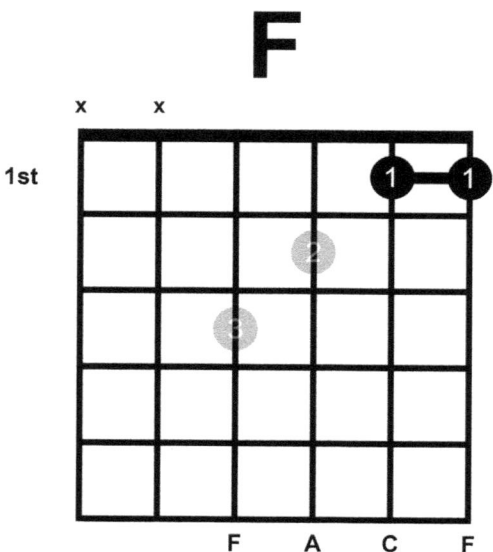

Fast Guitar Chord Transitions

Now move your second (2) and third (3) fingers directly onto the fretboard together. You'll still be on the third and second frets but now on the fourth (D) and third (G) strings. Strum across only the last four strings and you'll have the easy F chord. I typically use this chord rather than playing than the full six-string barre chord. It sounds just as good and is much quicker to get to. Practice going back and forth between C and F.

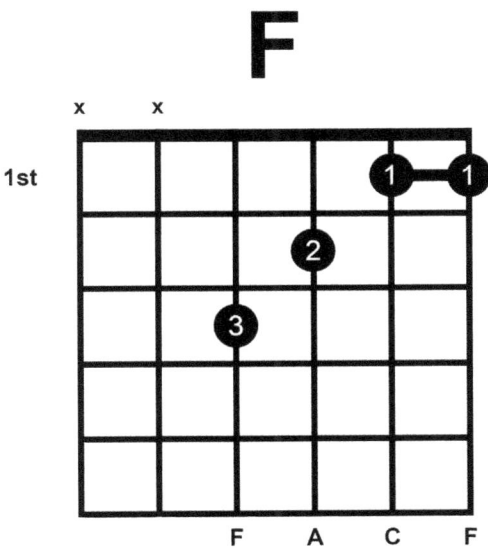

Micah Brooks

The Chords in "E"

The key of E has so many open chords in it!

One of the characteristics of the guitar is its ability to change chords while leaving some of the same notes in place. This is called *playing open*. You'll understand the concept more as you fret these chord. Playing open provides continuity of sound. Plus, it makes the transitions easier because you won't need to cover as many strings per move. The key of E is the champion of this approach.

E5 to Bsus

Likely you've learned how to play an E chord like this one on the next page.

Micah Brooks

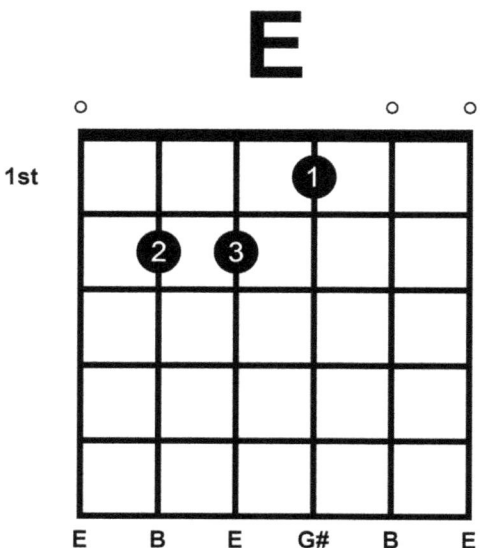

Try a new way to play E. Technically it's called an E5, but it transitions to Bsus smoothly and sounds great. I use this version of the E chord often when playing in the key of E. Your first (1) finger is on the seventh fret of the fifth (A) string. Your third (3) and fourth (4) fingers make a stretch up to the ninth frets of the fourth (D) and third (G) strings. Strum across all six strings–even the low sixth string (E).

Fast Guitar Chord Transitions

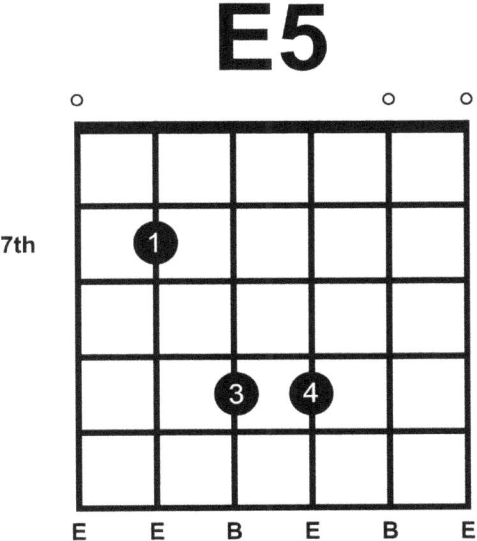

Each of the following two chords is going to look similar to the first E5 chord except for which fret number they fall on. To get to a Bsus chord, you only need to slide each finger down to the second and fourth frets. I emphasize sliding because your fingers do not need to come off the guitar. You'll only strum five strings this time. Leave out the low six (E) string.

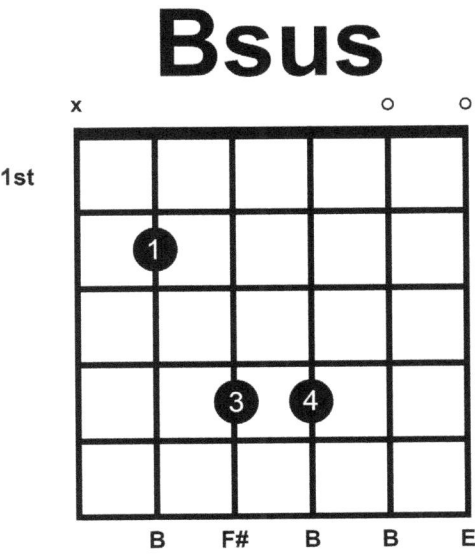

Bsus to C#m7

Moving from Bsus to C#m7 is as easy as moving from E5 to Bsus. You only need to slide up two frets. Your first (1) finger will move from the second fret of the fifth (A) string to the fourth. Each of your other two fingers slides with it.

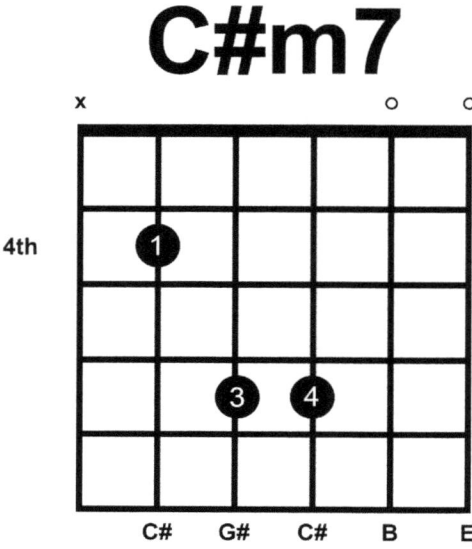

C#m7 to A2

Our next move is to slide from C#m7 to A2. You will notice that you'll still use your third (3) and fourth (4) fingers, but not your first (1) finger. As you slide from the fourth fret to an open string with your first finger (1) you'll feel like you're sliding off the guitar. Work on making that slide as smooth as possible.

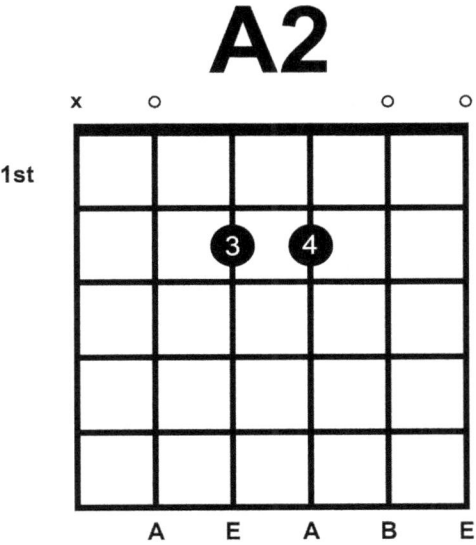

A2 to F#m7

Your final move in this key is extremely simple. Often you'll play an F#m7 while in the key of E. One way to make that happen is through a tougher barre chord. Another way–perhaps a better way– is simply to place your first (1) finger on the second fret of the sixth (E) string. Notice that you will need to mute the fifth (A) string. Your first (1) finger should naturally do this as you place it on the second fret of the sixth (E) string. It should lightly touch the fifth (A) string, thus dampening it or muting it. This makes such a quick transition between A2 and F#m7. Plus, your third (3) and fourth (4) fingers are still together making a transition to E5, C#m7, or Bsus quick as well. Practice going from F#m7 to all other chords in the key of E.

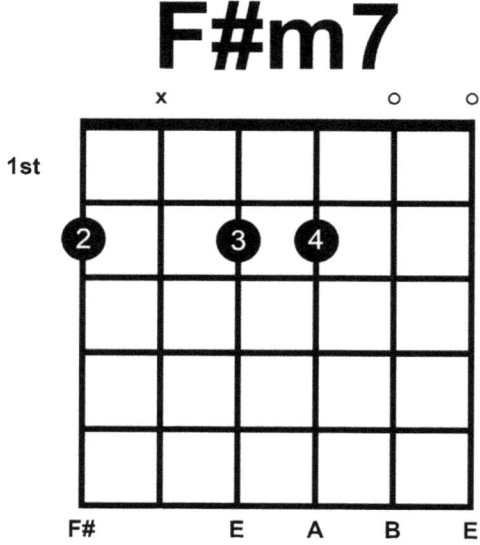

The Chords in "A"

Playing in A has a barre chord or two, but it's doable!

Our final key for this book is the key of A. Don't worry! The chapter after this one shows you how to take all five chapters and use them to play in any key you'd like.

The key of A is unique in that it has both open chords while using several of the staple guitar chords–such as A, E, and D.

A to E (using a new A fingering shape)

The A chord below is how you would typically play the chord.

Micah Brooks

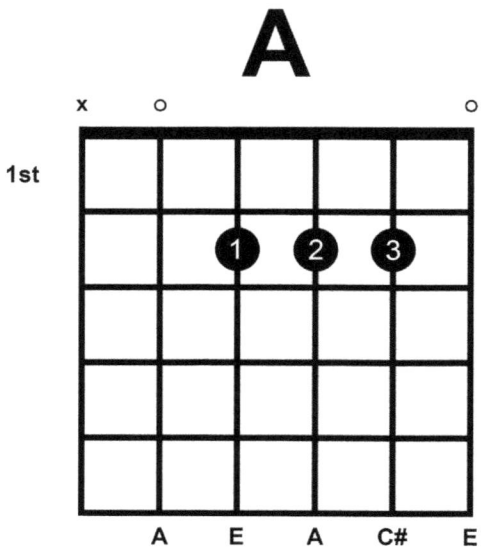

Try this new version of A that lets you get to an E chord much quicker. It involves a slide too. This would be impossible using the traditional fingering shape for an A chord.

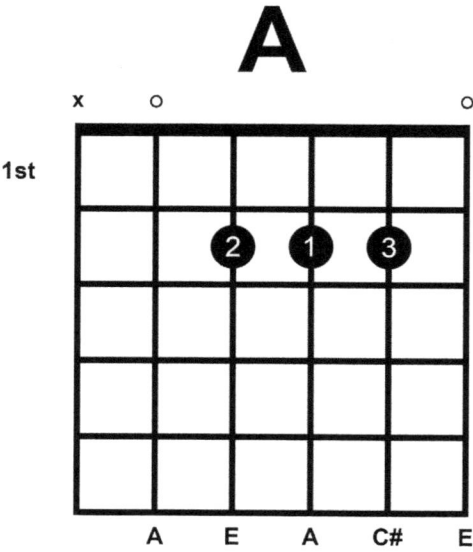

Fast Guitar Chord Transitions

Now we are going to make the slide from A to E. Let your first (1) finger take the lead in this transition.

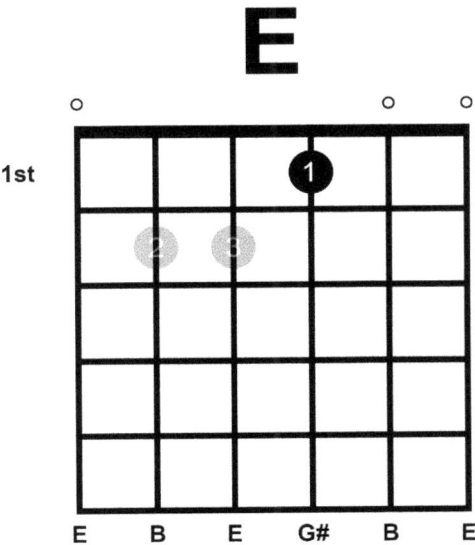

Your second (2) and third (3) fingers should now move as one package to the second frets of the fifth (A) and fourth (D) strings. You'll now be in the position to plan an E chord. Practice moving between the two chords. Use your first (1) finger as your slide (pivot) point as much as you can. This makes your transition speed up nicely.

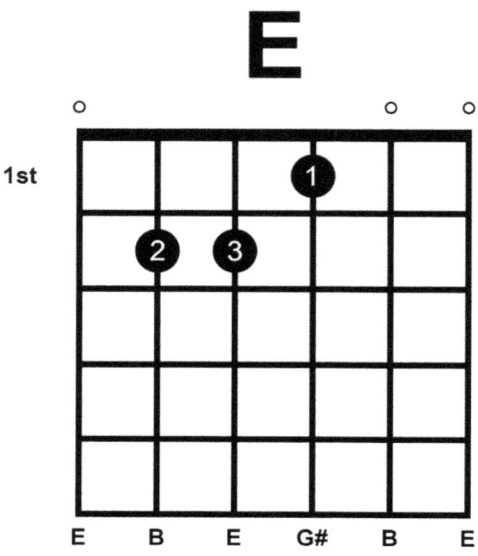

E to F#m

Admittedly, moving from an E chord to an F#m is hard. It's also necessary when playing in the key of A. There is no smooth slide from one fret to the next. Every finger has to move off the fretboard and land in an F#m shape. That said, when you first begin learning an F#m chord you may have built it in steps. First, you placed your first (1) finger across all six strings on the second fret. Then you likely placed your third (3) and fourth (4) fingers down on the fourth frets of the fifth (A) and fourth (D) strings. To speed up this transition make it your goal to move everything all at once—each finger moves into place at the same time. Likely this will take some time and effort to make this a one motion chord but I believe you are up to the challenge!

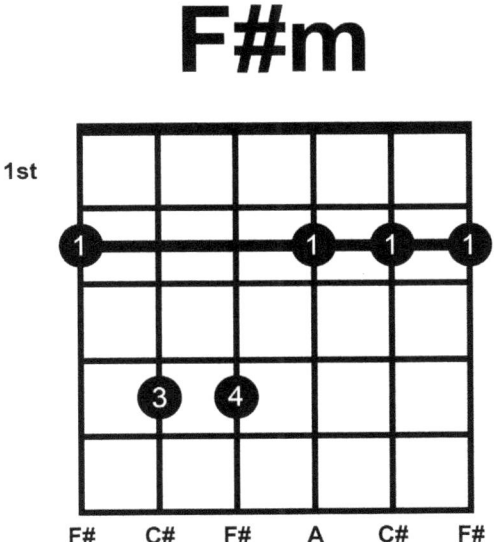

F#m to Bm

I've got good news for you! Especially so having come from a tough F#m chord. Often you'll move from F#m to Bm while in the key of A. This is such a simple move. Plus, it should be done in one swift motion. While fretting an F#m, move your first (1), third (3), and fourth (4) fingers down towards the ground a string each as you bring your second (2) finger onto the third fret of the second (B) string. You now only barre and strum across the last five strings.

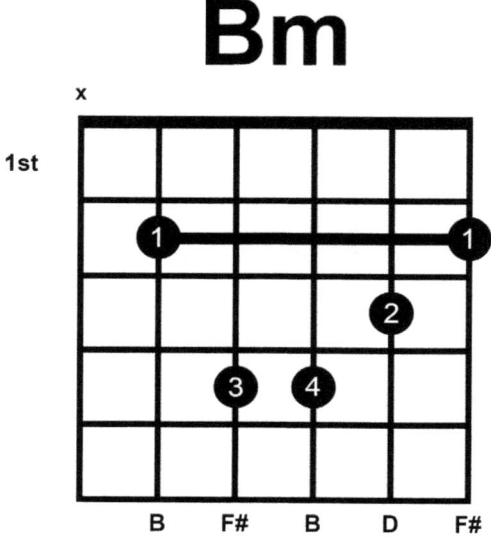

Bm to D

One final chord that works so well in the key of A is moving Bm to D. It's another chord transition that doesn't share any of the same fingers on the same frets but it's easy nonetheless. First, fret your Bm from the previous section. You'll notice that when moving to D three fingers can jump easily into place because they are in a similar shape while playing a Bm. You'll omit your fourth (4) finger for this chord. In one smooth motion move your first (1) finger onto the second fret of the third (G) string while moving your third (3) finger to the third fret of the second (B) string and your second (2) finger to the second fret of the first (e) string. This makes a D chord. Strum only the last four strings.

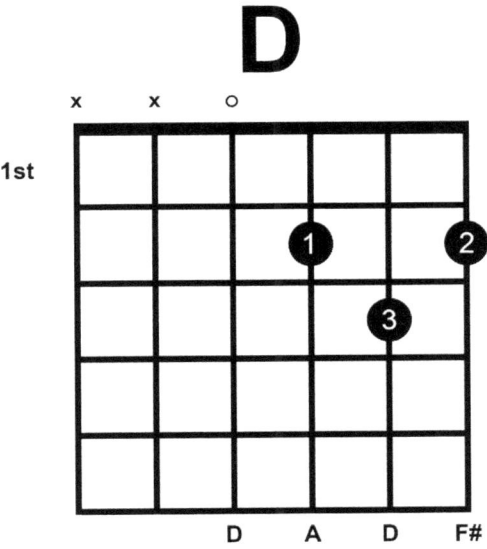

Micah Brooks

The Nashville Numbers System & The Mighty Capo

Music is math

This section is devoted to music theory. However, before you turn the page, I aim to give you the most applicable section of music theory that you will ever need. There will be no mention of accidentals or words like harmonic progression. Rather, I want to do my best to train you in practical music theory you can use every time you play the guitar. I use this stuff each time I pick up my guitar and so can you.

One more disclaimer, the method I propose next is basic. If you have music theory friends, they may either say "duh" or attempt to clutter this with more information. These are the basic building blocks for theory that all musicians need. This is not a comprehensive study. To do that, go to Belmont University in Nashville, TN where I went or another music school. They know it all there. This is for those of us in the trenches. This is for anyone who wants the basics so that you can get out there and perform.

Numbers

Music is built on notes. Notes join in series to create scales. The fundamental or root note of the scale is the tonic note. A chord is the addition of two or more notes played at the same time. Playing in a certain key means that you are playing music by the rules of particularly predefined tones that work well with one another. Every key has a fundamental or root chord. This is the **1 chord**. The 1 chord is the foundation for the other chords coming next in what I will call the *chord scale*.

There is a more in-depth section below explaining what is under the hood of each of the following chords. This is a bird's eye perspective for understanding how chords relate one to another. If you can understand this section then you will be able to hear and play just about any pop or worship song you want.

Building from the 1 chord we spoke about above, the 4 and 5 chords relate most solidly with the 1 chord. Because this is a guitar book, let me use the key of G as an example throughout the rest of this section. It will help if you play these chords while you read along to hear the differences mentioned. In the key of G, the 1 chord is G. You guessed it! The 4 chord is the C chord and the 5 chord is D. These numbers are the three pillar chords in any key that are the structural triangle from which all the others derive. While the 1 chord is dominant, the 4 and 5 are also equally important chords in any key.

Next, the 2m and the 6m chords derive from the 4 and 1 chords, respectively. The 2m7 and 6m7 are simply 4 and 1 chords with their bass notes shifted down the scale two notes. In the key of G, the 2m chord is an Am and the 6m is an Em. If you have played much in the key of G then you know how important these two chords are to most songs.

Moving forward, music theory would say that the 3m and 7dim (diminished) are the final chords you should learn when learning these types of major chord scales. Practically though, you will rarely play a 3m or 7dim. Especially in popular music. Instead, I recommend learning the 1/3 and 5/7 chords. These are chords with shifted up bass notes, by the amount of two steps, from both the 1 chord and the 5 chord. In the case of the key of G, these chords would be 1/3 = G/B and the 5/7 = D/F#. I imagine that you have seen these chords before. They are foundational.

Basic chord theory - Let's drill this down

I am going to drill down into each chord number and how each triad is built. I will do my best not to lose you. I hope to give you insight into being able to see chord relationships and how each interacts one to another. The goal is for you to be a better guitarist. Knowing this stuff will increase that likelihood.

Each of these little sections assumes we are building from the foundational 1 chord. Music theorists can, and some will, make this more complicated. Do your best to stay focused and keep using the key of G examples throughout.

1 Chord

The 1 chord, as noted before, is foundational and fundamental. It is the chord to which we will reference most of the other chords. It is like the President of the United States. Sure, the Vice President is important but less so than the President. The 1 chord is built on the triad of 1, 3, and 5 notes in the major scale. Please understand that throughout the rest of this chapter, we now assume a major scale. There are several other scales we could use, but for popular music, the major scale is the most played. In the key of G, the 1 chord is the G chord and is built using the notes G, B, and D. You can rearrange those letters however you would like (called inversions) and you will still have a G chord.

4 Chord

The 4 chord shares one very important note with the 1 chord, which is the root note G. A 4 chord, using the same scale as from the 1 chord, is built as 1, 4, 6. The root position for this chord, however, would really be 4, 6, and 1. The 4 being the root note of the 4 chord. In the key of G example, the 4 is a C chord and is built C, E, and G. Thus, the G note (which is the tonic note of the G scale) is shared between these two chords. This helps them to be related in music.

5 Chord

The 5 chord shares one important note with the 1 chord, as the 4 did, but this time it is the 5 note, rather than the 1. This makes this chord have an opposing sound to the 1 chord. Whereas the 4 chord sounds more complementary. A 5 chord is built as 5, 7, 2. 5 is the root note of this chord. In the key of G, this is the D chord and these notes would be D, F#, and A. Again, rearrange those notes however you would like and you still have a D chord.

2m Chord

The 2m chord is interestingly a 4 chord where the bass note is shifted down two steps. Technically the 2m7 is the 4 chord shifted, but the purpose is the same—I digress. A 2m chord is built as the 2, 4, and 6 notes in the scale. Remember, a 4 chord is a 1, 4, and 6. The 2m chord in the key of G is Am. The notes are A, C, and E.

6m Chord

The 6m chord is one used in just about every pop song. It is as famous as the 1, 4, and 5 chords. Like the 2m, the 6m is a derivative of an important chord. The 6m and the 1 chord are almost the same. The 6m7 is made of the same notes as a 1 chord, but the bass note is shifted downward two steps. In the key of G, the Em is the 6m. If you have played much in the key of G then you have played an Em. Those notes are E, G, and B.

1/3 Chord

A 1/3 is just as it sounds: a full 1 chord with this bass note shifted up to a 3 note. The 1 chord being a 1, 3, 5 and then the shifted bass note being a 3. In the key of G, this chord is a G/B. Those notes are B, D, and G. This chord has a sense of movement or motion to it. What that means is that typically you will play this chord on the way to the next one. It's also called a passing chord. Whereas with a 1, 4, or 5 chord you may rest measures or most of a verse/chorus on one or two of these chords. I cannot think of a time where I have spent more than one or two measures on a 1/3. Again, it has the sense of transition or motion to it.

5/7 Chord

Extremely similar to the 1/3, the 5/7 chord is simply a 5 chord with a shifted up 7 note in the bass. Another passing chord, these notes are 7, 2, and 5. In the key of G this is a D/F# chord and is built F#, A, and D. This chord is used often to transition from the 1 chord, G, to the 6m chord, Em.

What is a capo and why it's not cheating?

When you research the word *capo* on dictionary.com you find that the capo is the chief of a branch of the Mafia. Wait...no. That's not the definition of capo that we are looking for. Rather, a capo is a device that when clamped or screwed down across the strings on any given fret will raise each string a corresponding number of halftones. To put this a little more applicably, a capo allows you to play what should have been barre chords but using open chords–easier chords–instead. Remember, open chords tend to sound stronger than barre chords and sustain longer.

Some say that using a capo is a form of cheating. The use of the guitar capo is not a cheat in any manner. Your capo is a tool that allows you to expand the abilities of your playing.

The guitar was meant to be played with as many variations of open chords as possible. An open chord assumes there is at least one string that is left untouched allowing it to resonate openly. With any instrument, more resonance produces better quality sound.

Let's use the numbers we learned from the previous section to play in keys with open positions. Normally the key would be played using barre chord versions.

Chord Families

Key	1	2m	1/3	4	5	6m	5/7	1
G	G	Am	G/B	C	D	Em	D/F#	G
A♭	A♭	B♭m	A♭/C	D♭	E♭	Fm	E♭/G	A♭
A	A	Bm	A/C#	D	E	F#m	E/G#	A
B♭	B♭	Cm	B♭/D	E♭	F	Gm	F/A	B♭
B	B	C#m	B/D#	E	F#	G#m	F#/A#	B
C	C	Dm	C/E	F	G	Am	G/B	C
D♭	D♭	E♭m	D♭/F	G♭	A♭	B♭m	A♭/C	D♭
D	D	Em	D/F#	G	A	Bm	A/C#	D
E♭	E♭	Fm	E♭/G	A♭	B♭	Cm	B♭/D	E♭
E	E	F#m	E/G#	A	B	C#m	B/D#	E
F	F	Gm	F/A	B♭	C	Dm	C/E	F
G♭	G♭	A♭m	G♭/B♭	C♭ (B)	D♭	E♭m	D♭/F	G♭

This is where math comes into play. The diagram above shows every natural and sharp/flat major key and the corresponding number of chords that you will use to do some head math while transposing using your capo. If this is the first time you have ever tried to transpose music in your head please give yourself time to learn this. I use this trick every time I play guitar on stage. Understanding these numbers and how they integrate one to another is the key to being charts/sheet-music-free on stage. I have a friend who plays bass by understanding these numbers and has a catalog of songs he has memorized that has to be well over 5000. If he did not know how to do this type of chord number head math those 5000 songs would need to be written down.

Popular keys to use with the capo and why

This section details some of the most important and often used capo positions and why most guitarists use them. Please understand that there are well over one hundred ways to use the capo in a normal fashion. I wouldn't describe each one of them or you might fall asleep. I can't have that! Rather, I am outlining my favorites and the ones I use just about every guitar session.

Using the capo while playing in the key of G

A long time ago someone must have been dreaming that he or she could play in the key of G but use those chord shapes to play in the many other keys found on the guitar. The capo allows you to do just that. If you place the capo on the fourth fret and play using the key of G chords you are now effectively playing in the key of B. This is huge! Playing in B otherwise would include several tough to play barre chords. Not so with a capo on the fourth fret and the key of G!

Depending on your guitar, it may be best to place your capo either exactly in the middle of the frets or on the upper third of the frets. Some guitars favor the middle; some the upper third.

The diagram below gives you the key of G transpositions for every key up to the tenth fret. Anything higher than the tenth fret and you should just buy a mandolin. A few of my favorites you could try are capoing the second fret to play in the key of A, capoing the fifth fret to play in C and capoing the seventh fret to play in D.

Capo Using the Key of G

Capo Number	1	2m	1/3	4	5	6m	5/7	1
Open	G	Am	G/B	C	D	Em	D/F#	G
Capo 1	A♭	B♭m	A♭/C	D♭	E♭	Fm	E♭/G	A♭
Capo 2	A	Bm	A/C#	D	E	F#m	E/G#	A
Capo 3	B♭	Cm	B♭/D	E♭	F	Gm	F/A	B♭
Capo 4	B	C#m	B/D#	E	F#	G#m	F#/A#	B
Capo 5	C	Dm	C/E	F	G	Am	G/B	C
Capo 6	D♭	E♭m	D♭/F	G♭	A♭	B♭m	A♭/C	D♭
Capo 7	D	Em	D/F#	G	A	Bm	A/C#	D
Capo 8	E♭	Fm	E♭/G	A♭	B♭	Cm	B♭/D	E♭
Capo 9	E	F#m	E/G#	A	B	C#m	B/D#	E
Capo 10	F	Gm	F/A	B♭	C	Dm	C/E	F

Using the capo while playing in the key of D

The second chord most guitar players learn after the chord "G" is "D". "D" is beautiful and only four strings. The power in this chord is that the third note of the scale is at the top of the chord. Depending on the melody and type of the song, having the third note at the top of the chord may be the perfect sound for what you are trying to accomplish. Using the capo with the key of D positions allows you to keep that third note at the top of the chord, but playing in normally barre chord keys or open keys, but different positioning. For instance, if you apply the capo to the first fret and play in "D" you are now effectively playing in the key of E♭. Playing a "D" to "A" to "G" with the capo on the first fret allows you to really be playing an "E♭" to "B♭" to "A♭" chords. Try each of those using barre chords and your fingers get tired and–more importantly–your chord sustain is diminished. Move your capo up one fret to the second fret and you are playing in the key of E. Move it up to fret four and you are playing in G♭. Up one more fret and you are playing in the key of G. Try taking the capo off the guitar and playing in the normal, open chord version of the key of G then compare it with the capo five version using the key of D chords. These are two different ways to play in the same key. One is not better than the other. They are both options depending on the sound of music you want to make. These are called inversions–just like pianists use.

Capo Using the Key of D

Capo Number	1	2m	1/3	4	5	6m	5/7	1
Open	D	Em	D/F#	G	A	Bm	A/C#	D
Capo 1	E♭	Fm	E♭/G	A♭	B♭	Cm	B♭/D	E♭
Capo 2	E	F#m	E/G#	A	B	C#m	B/D#	E
Capo 3	F	Gm	F/A	B♭	C	Dm	C/E	F
Capo 4	G♭	A♭m	G♭/B♭	C♭ (B)	D♭	E♭m	D♭/F	G♭
Capo 5	G	Am	G/B	C	D	Em	D/F#	G
Capo 6	A♭	B♭m	A♭/C	D♭	E♭	Fm	E♭/G	A♭
Capo 7	A	Bm	A/C#	D	E	F#m	E/G#	A
Capo 8	B♭	Cm	B♭/D	E♭	F	Gm	F/A	B♭
Capo 9	B	C#m	B/D#	E	F#	G#m	F#/A#	B
Capo 10	C	Dm	C/E	F	G	Am	G/B	C

Using the capo while playing in the key of C

Place your capo across the fifth frets (again, either in the middle or upper third depending on what your guitar prefers) and play in the key of C. You have effectively transposed to the key of F. Use the key of C to play in a variety of other keys. Yes, you'll need to use an F chord, but we worked on a much easier F than the harder barre version earlier.

Use the diagram below to play in as many keys as you would like using the key of C and your capo. Some of my favorites are capo 2 in D, capo 4 in E and capo 7 in G. Playing in the key of C with a capo is also a great way to play in sharp (#) and flat (♭) keys. I especially love the sound of capo 1 in D♭ and capo 3 in E♭.

Capo Using the Key of C

Capo Number	1	2m	1/3	4	5	6m	5/7	1
Open	C	Dm	C/E	F	G	Am	G/B	C
Capo 1	D♭	E♭m	D♭/F	G♭	A♭	B♭m	A♭/C	D♭
Capo 2	D	Em	D/F#	G	A	Bm	A/C#	D
Capo 3	E♭	Fm	E♭/G	A♭	B♭	Cm	B♭/D	E♭
Capo 4	E	F#m	E/G#	A	B	C#m	B/D#	E
Capo 5	F	Gm	F/A	B♭	C	Dm	C/E	F
Capo 6	G♭	A♭m	G♭/B♭	C♭ (B)	D♭	E♭m	D♭/F	G♭
Capo 7	G	Am	G/B	C	D	Em	D/F#	G
Capo 8	A♭	B♭m	A♭/C	D♭	E♭	Fm	E♭/G	A♭
Capo 9	A	Bm	A/C#	D	E	F#m	E/G#	A
Capo 10	B♭	Cm	B♭/D	E♭	F	Gm	F/A	B♭

Using the capo while playing in the key of E

The guitar loves the key of E. The reason is simple and plain to hear. The key of E uses the lowest notes (in standard tuning) that the guitar allows. The key of E growls. When you add the capo to the mix you can borrow the open nature of E, but use it for some often barre chord keys, like the key of G♭. Place your capo on the second fret and play in the key of E. You are now playing in the key of G♭ when you play the chords B, C#m, and A. The power of this key is that the root note E is at the top of all of these chords. Add the capo to the third fret and play in E, you are now playing in the key of G. Yes, the guitar is made to play in G without a capo, but this technique broadens the types of open chords you can play. It is just another way to play in the same key. Add the capo to the fifth fret to play in A. Move it up two more frets to the seventh fret to play in the key of B. Move up one more fret to the eighth fret and you are now in the key of C.

Capo Using the Key of E

Capo Number	1	2m	1/3	4	5	6m	5/7	1
Open	E	F#m	E/G#	A	B	C#m	B/D#	E
Capo 1	F	Gm	F/A	B♭	C	Dm	C/E	F
Capo 2	G♭	A♭m	G♭/B♭	C♭ (B)	D♭	E♭m	D♭/F	G♭
Capo 3	G	Am	G/B	C	D	Em	D/F#	G
Capo 4	A♭	B♭m	A♭/C	D♭	E♭	Fm	E♭/G	A♭
Capo 5	A	Bm	A/C#	D	E	F#m	E/G#	A
Capo 6	B♭	Cm	B♭/D	E♭	F	Gm	F/A	B♭
Capo 7	B	C#m	B/D#	E	F#	G#m	F#/A#	B
Capo 8	C	Dm	C/E	F	G	Am	G/B	C
Capo 9	D♭	E♭m	D♭/F	G♭	A♭	B♭m	A♭/C	D♭
Capo 10	D	Em	D/F#	G	A	Bm	A/C#	D

Micah Brooks

Using the capo while playing in the key of A

The chords used on the guitar to play in the key of A are very helpful. In this key about 80% of the chords are open. This brings stability to the key and it sounds wonderful to the ear. Using the capo while playing in A allows you to use the key of A's open sound, but in keys that would normally be barre chord keys. Place your capo on the second fret. When you now play an A to an E chord you are playing a B to an F#. Depending on your song, this can be a great way to play in the key of B. This is especially true if the melody lands on the 5th note of the scale often. Place your capo on the third fret and play in A to play in the key of C. Now move it up to the fifth fret to play in the key of D.

Capo Using the Key of A

Capo Number	1	2m	1/3	4	5	6m	5/7	1
Open	A	Bm	A/C#	D	E	F#m	E/G#	A
Capo 1	B♭	Cm	B♭/D	E♭	F	Gm	F/A	B♭
Capo 2	B	C#m	B/D#	E	F#	G#m	F#/A#	B
Capo 3	C	Dm	C/E	F	G	Am	G/B	C
Capo 4	D♭	E♭m	D♭/F	G♭	A♭	B♭m	A♭/C	D♭
Capo 5	D	Em	D/F#	G	A	Bm	A/C#	D
Capo 6	E♭	Fm	E♭/G	A♭	B♭	Cm	B♭/D	E♭
Capo 7	E	F#m	E/G#	A	B	C#m	B/D#	E
Capo 8	F	Gm	F/A	B♭	C	Dm	C/E	F
Capo 9	G♭	A♭m	G♭/B♭	C♭ (B)	D♭	E♭m	D♭/F	G♭
Capo 10	G	Am	G/B	C	D	Em	D/F#	G

Closing Thoughts and Finding Songs to Play

You've just crossed the finish line!

You've made it! You've acquired the stills needed to accomplish several important guitar chord transitions! It's time to put them to good use. You could consider joining a band, finding some friends to jam with, or auditioning for your church's worship team. You're so good now that you'd be a gem in any group.

If you'd like to keep finding more instruction material, I recommend my book, *Guitar Secrets Revealed*. While it's for the intermediate guitar player, I think you're right on track! You'll learn how the guitar pro's think. You learned transitions with this book. With the next one, you'll learn new chords; new ways to use some of the chords you already know; and the professional mindset that is invaluable longterm.

Beyond that, you need some songs to play!

I'm betting that you'd love some resources to help you learn some new songs. After all, we now have an arsenal of chords with which to use. Here are three that I recommend. They are fakebooks, the internet, and something called *guitar chords*.

Fakebooks are better known as lead sheets but were coined *fakebooks* several years ago. A lead sheet has chords written on top of a melody line. While you have to do some work to figure out when to play each chord, they are succinct ways of fitting an entire song on two or three pages. You can purchase fakebooks on Amazon.com or wherever sheet music is typically sold in your area.

Another resource is the internet. The internet is filled with vast amounts of written music that you can play. There is a wide spectrum of content qualities too. You could buy professionally transcribed full scores (where every note is written out) to *Back-Woods-Johnny's version of a song he transcribed in his basement*. A quick search using the term "[song title] sheet music" should produce several ways to play the song you're looking for.

You could also search for the term "[song title] guitar chords". A guitar chord chart, or just a *chord chart*, includes the chords written atop the lyrics. This is also a succinct way to transcribe a song. It's critical to mention that *Johnny in his basement* may be able to publish some chord charts on his webpage, but the chords may not always be accurate. These are his best guesses as to what the chords should be. As a beginner/intermediate player, you should consider purchasing your sheet music, lead sheets, or chord charts. This way you'll know that the chords are correct. Plus, you'll know that the writers of the music are being properly compensated. A great guitar chord website is ultimate-guitar.com.

Thank you for trusting me to teach you some of the basics of the guitar. I hope that you plan to continue learning and I believe you can be successful. Strum away!

About The Author

Why so many people learn music from Micah

The best instructors teach to the student, not to the curriculum. The curriculum serves as a vehicle for learning. It's a tool of sorts. One of the best parts of teaching music lessons–in this case, guitar chording–is the ability to help a student learn at just the right pace. I've found that my job as an educator is to always be encouraging my students to take one step more than he or she may not have taken on their own. The only thing to sort out is at which pace each student performs best.

I've been teaching guitar and piano courses for more than ten years. My emphasis has always been, and will likely always be, in commercial music. While I think classical music is worth studying, I always find myself improvising over the original melodies–even those of the greats, like Beethoven, Brahms, or Bach. It's human nature to explore or be curious and I love teaching with the mindset that the music greats of the past are like proven guides. They shouldn't always be copied, but rather those from whom to learn.

Living twenty-five miles from downtown Nashville, TN has provided myself and family privileges in music that I'm certain are not given in every town. You can't throw a stone in Nashville without hitting someone who is personally or has a family member in the music industry. Not one of us takes the Grand Ole Opry backstage tour because we all plan to be there as an artist someday. Even if we sing and play music for Jesus as Christian or worship artists, we still likely won't spend the time or money for that tour. We plan to perform on that ageless circle that lands center-stage someday ourselves.

My wife of more than ten years is glowing brighter every year. We have four kids who keep us very busy and quite exhausted! We also keep two Yorkshire Terrier dogs who I'm sure my wife would give away for less than the price of two movie tickets. I love them though.

It's an honor to help you work toward your guitar chording goals. These new methods may unlock creativity in you that has been buried deep within for years. It's time to let it out.

Blessings,

-Micah Brooks
www.micahbrooks.com
Find me on Facebook, Twitter, LinkedIn, Instagram, and Amazon.com

Connect With Micah Brooks

Signup for Micah Brooks emails to stay up to date

Subscribe to the Micah Brooks Company "Stay Connected" email list for the latest book releases. This email list is always free and intended to deliver high-value content to your inbox. Visit the link below to signup.

www.micahbrooks.com

Contact Micah

Email Micah Brooks at micahbrooks.com/contact. I want to know who you are. It's my privilege to respond to your emails personally. Please feel free to connect.

Please share this book with your friends

If you would like to share your thanks for this book, the best thing you can do is to tell a friend about *Fast Guitar Chord Transitions* or buy them a copy. You can also show your appreciation for this book by leaving a review on Amazon:

www.amazon.com

Follow Micah Brooks:

Facebook: @micahbrooksofficial
Twitter: @micahbrooksco
LinkedIn: Micah Brooks
Instagram: @micahbrooksco
Amazon: amazon.com/author/micahbrooks

If you have trouble connecting to any of these social media accounts, please visit www.micahbrooks.com.

Worship Publishing is a resource website that includes books, daily devotions, music, podcasts, product reviews, and many more recommendations. Use our wealth of staff writers and high-quality guest post content to better your walk with the Lord. This is the website where you can find publishing information for WorshipHeart Publishing, the publisher of this book. Visit: www.worshippublishing.com.

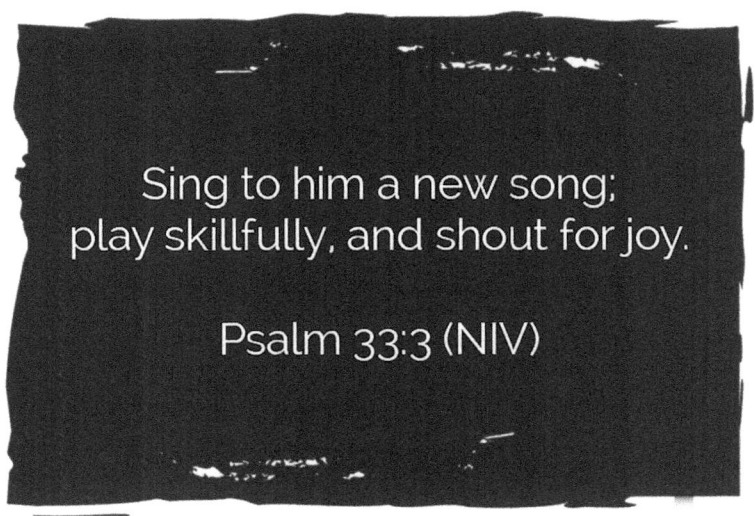